RICHARD HEF

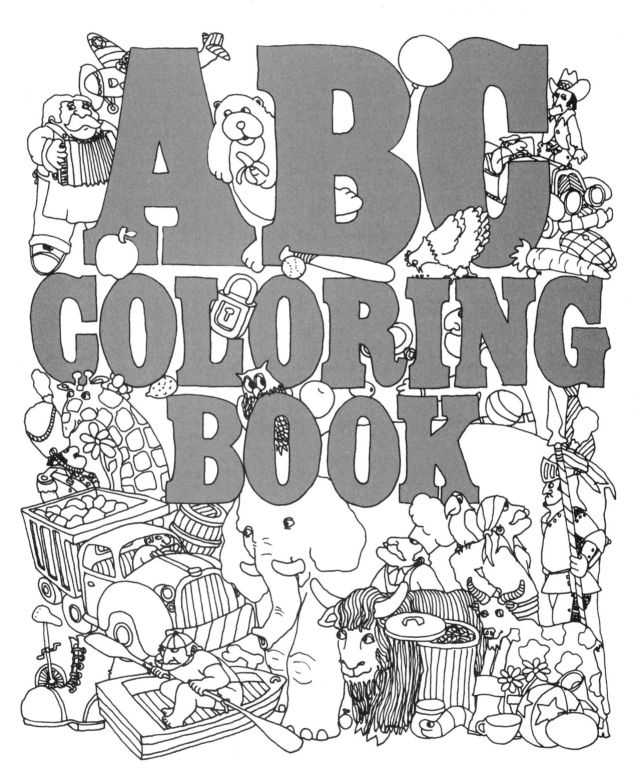

Dover Publications, Inc., New York

Publisher's Note

In Mr. Hefter's zany illustrated alphabet, A stands for the traditional Apple, of course, but also for Abacus, Apron, Accordionist, Anchor and 13 other amusing and elusive objects.

At the bottom of each page we list the objects pictured that begin with the appropriate letter. But in order not to spoil your fun in discovering these things by yourself, we have made them a little difficult to read by printing them upside down; the number right side up and in parentheses tells you how many objects you can hope to find. If you look hard enough and use enough imagination, you may find even more!

Copyright

Copyright © 1973 by Dover Publications, Inc.
All rights reserved.

Bibliographical Note

ABC Coloring Book is a new work, first published by Dover Publications, Inc., in 1973. The original line drawings were prepared especially for this edition by Richard Hefter.

International Standard Book Number

ISBN-13: 978-0-486-22969-0
ISBN-10: 0-486-22969-6

Manufactured in the United States by Courier Corporation
22969624
www.doverpublications.com

(18 A's)

abacus, accordion, accordionist, acrobat, airplane, alligator, anchor, ankle, apple, apron, archer, arm, armchair, arrow, asp, aviator, axe, axle.

bag, ball, balloon, banana, barbell, barber pole, barn, barrel, baseball, bat, beanie,
bear, beard, bell, belt, berries, bicycle, bird, boat, bone, bottle, bowl, box, bread,
butterfly.

(25 B's)

cabin, cake, candles, cap, car, carrot, cat, celery, chair, chaps, cheese, cherries, chicken, chimney, chin, circle, clouds, coat, coffeepot, collar, cook, corn, cow, cowboy, crown, cuffs, cup, curtains.

(28 C's)

(19 D's)

daisies, dart, dentist, dentures, doctor, dog (dalmatian), doll, door, doorbell, doorknob, doormat, dots, dress, drill, driver, drum, drummer, drumsticks, dumptruck.

eagle, ears, eel, egg, egg beater, eggplant, eggshells, egg white, egg yolk, elbow, elephant, emperor, envelope, eskimo, eyebrow, eyes. (16 E's)

face, farmer, fence, fiddle, fiddler, fingers, fire, fire engine, fire hose, fire hydrant,
firemen, fish, fish tank, flag, flagpole, flame, football, forest, fountain, fruit, frying pan,
funnel.

(22 F's)

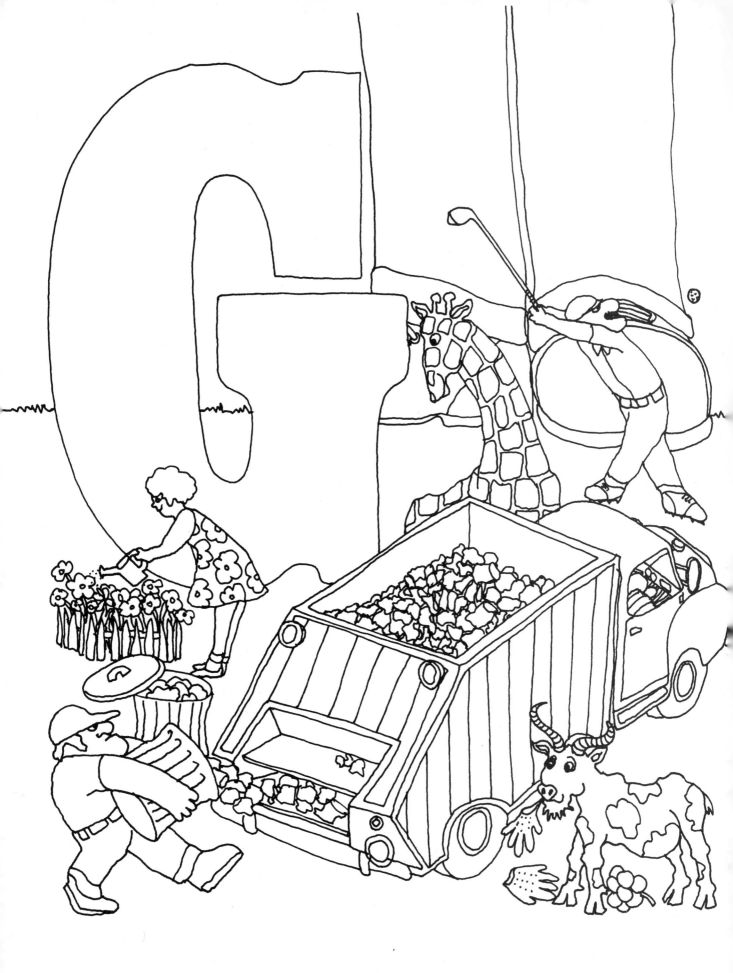

garbage, garbage cans, garbage man, garbage truck, garden, gardener, giant, giraffe, girl, gloves, goat, golf ball, golf club, golfer, grapes, grass. (16 G's) hair, hammer, handle, hands, harness, hat, head, heart, heel, helicopter, helmet, hippopotamus, hook, hooves, horizon, horn, horse, house.

(18 H's)

iceberg, ice bucket, ice cream, ice cubes, ice pick, ice skates, icicle, iguana, inchworm, Indian, initial, ink, ink spot, insects, iron, island, ivy.

(17 I's)

jacket, jack-in-the-box, jack-o'-lantern, jackrabbit, jacks, jam, janitor, jars, jeep, jester, jet pilot, jet plane, jewelry, jug, juggling, juice, juicer, jumping beans, jump rope.

(19 J's)

kangaroo, kayak, kettle, key, keyhole, king, kite, kitten, knee, knife, knight, knob, knockwurst, knot, knuckles.

laces, ladder, ladybug, lamb, lamp, lampshade, lantern, lapel, laundry, laundry basket,
leaf, legs, lemon, light, limb, lion, lion tamer, lips, lock, locks (of hair), locomotive,
log, lollipop, lumberjack, lunchbox.

mailbox, mallet, man, map, marbles, medal, melon, milk, milkman, mirror, mole, monkey, moon, moose, motor, motorcycle, mountain, mouse, moustache, muffins, mushrooms.

(27 M's)

nails, name, nametag, neck, necktie, needle, nest, net, nine, nipple, noodles, Norman,
nose, nostril, number, nurse, nutcracker, nuts, nutshells.

(19 N's)

oar, obelisk, ocean, ocean liner, oil, oilcan, octopus, olive, opera singer, orange, organ, organist, ostrich, overalls, overcoat, owl.   (16 O's)

pad, pancakes, pants, paper, parachute, parachutist, parking meter, parrot, peanut, pear, peas, pencil, phone, pineapple, pirate, pistol, pitcher, plate, pocket, pod, pogo stick, pole, policeman, pot, potato, pumpkin, puppet, puppy. (28 P's)

quail, quart, quarterback, quarter, queen, question mark, quill, quilt, quiver, quotation marks.

(11 Q's)

rabbit, raccoon, race, race car, racetrack, railing, rain, rainbow, rain cloud, ram, rat, razor blade, referee, reindeer, rhinoceros, riders, ring, rocket, roller coaster, rooster, rope, rowboat, rower, runner.

(24 R's)

saddle, sail, sailboat, sailor, salt, saltshaker, sand, sand castle, saw, sawhorse, scales,
scissors, sea, sheep, shoes, shore, sky, slacks, smoke, snail, snorkel, squirrel, starfish,
steps, stirrups, sun, swimmer.

(27 S's)

table, tablecloth, tail, tank, target, tassel, tea bag, teacup, teapot, teaspoon, teeth, tepee, tie, tiger, tires, toast, toaster, toast, toenails, toes, tomato, tongue, toothbrush, toothpick, top, toy, tread, trees, triangle, truck, trumpet, tuna, turban, turret, turtle, typewriter.

(35 T's)

ukulele, umbrella, umpire, Uncle Sam, underpants, undershirt, unicycle, uniform, Union Jack. (9 U's)

vacuum cleaner, valley, vampire, vat, vegetables, vest, Viking, village, vine, violin, violinist, vise, vulture.

(13 V's)

wall, walrus, wart, wand, wastebasket, watch, water, water bucket, watermelon,
weather vane, well, wheel, wheelbarrow, whistle, whistle, windmill, window, witch, wood,
woodpecker, woodsman, work boots, worm.

(22 W's)

Xmas presents, Xmas tree, x-ray, xylophone, xylophonist.

(5 X's)

yacht, yachtsman, yak, yam, yardstick, yawn, yeoman, yoghurt, yogi, yoke, yolk.

zebra, zeppelin, zero, zigzag, zipper, zoo, zoo keeper.   (7 Z's)